Food, teeth and eating

A brief history

TODAY... 1978 Alison Paul and D. Southgate invent a scientific way of finding how much fibre there is in food, leading to a better understanding of how fibre is important to healthy eating... 1940 The McDonald brothers in California set up the first McDonalds hamburger restaurant. It will grow into an empire selling billions of hamburgers each year... 1924 Clarence Birdseye begins selling frozen foods after seeing how Eskimos preserve fish frozen in blocks of ice... 1906 Sir Frederick Hopkins discovers vitamins... 1894 Max Rubner shows that the body gets its energy from food. This energy, used by the body, is the same as when the food is burned. The energy in food can now be measured in units of heat called calories... 1865 German scientist, Karl von Voit studies how food is turned into energy... 1809 In France, Nicolas Appert invents the method of preserving food we now call canning. He also invents the stock cube... 1802 Geradus Mulder of Holland studies the materials that the body uses to build its tissues, and calls them proteins... 1765 In Italy, Lazzaro Spallanzani suggests that food will not go bad if it is sealed in airtight containers... 1728 Pierre Fauchard, in France, begins to use the metals tin, lead and gold for tooth fillings... 3000 BC The first false teeth are made in Sumer, in the Middle East, using wood, ivory and other locally available materials.

For more information... curriculumvisions.com

Word list

These are some science words that you should look out for as you go through the book. They are shown using CAPITAL letters.

CEREAL
A plant that produces grains that we can eat, for example wheat, rice and maize.

DAIRY PRODUCTS
Foods that are made mainly from milk, such as cheese and butter.

DIET
The food that you normally eat (not a special kind of food).

DIGESTIVE SYSTEM
The part of the body that extracts nourishment from food and passes it to the blood. The digestive system includes the stomach and intestine, often called the gut.

ENAMEL
The hard coating that surrounds a tooth.

ENERGY
The power in food, locked away as chemicals. We use it when we want to be active.

FAT
A substance that the body makes in order to store energy.

FIBRE
'Stringy' materials that make up much of a plant, but which we cannot digest.

FLAVOUR
The combination of taste and smell that occurs when you put something in your mouth.

FRUIT
The part of a plant containing seeds, such as apples, oranges and grapes.

GRAIN
The seeds of a cereal plant.

MILK TEETH
The first set of teeth. They are replaced by permanent teeth during childhood.

MINERALS
Naturally occurring chemicals, such as calcium and iron, that the body uses to build other chemicals.

PLAQUE
A sticky film on the teeth in which sugary foods can be changed to acids that cause tooth decay.

PROTEIN
The body-building substance in food.

STARCH
The main energy-rich part of plants such as cereals.

TEETH
Very hard peg-like bones that fit into the jaw. They have varying shapes for cutting, gripping and crushing.

TRADITIONAL FOOD
The food that people prepare from what is available locally.

VEGETABLE
A plant food eaten primarily for the vitamins in its leaves and roots.

VEGETARIAN
A person who chooses not to include meat in their diet.

VITAMINS
Chemicals that are essential to health. They are easily destroyed by cooking or storing food. That is why fresh food is so essential.

Contents

Weblink: www.CurriculumVisions.com

Food from around the world

People all over the world make tasty meals using different kinds of food. These foods provide nourishment even though they look very different.

We all have to eat. But, when you look across the world, you find that people eat very different things.

This is partly because some people live where it is warm and others live where it is cool, some live where it is wet and others where it is dry.

The same food plants and animals will not grow everywhere. So, over the generations, people have learned to use local plants and animals to make their meals (Pictures 1 to 3). These are called **TRADITIONAL FOODS**.

More recently, these different kinds of food have become available all over the world.

Different and equally healthy

Wherever people live in the world, they can usually stay healthy by eating what is grown or reared locally. To understand why this is so, we need to think about what is inside each type of food, not just what it looks or tastes like. That is what we will do on the next pages.

▶ **(Picture 1)** People who live in central America might make this meal. The yellow 'star' is made of tortilla chips. The tortilla chips are made from maize. In the centre is a mixture of beans and meat. This part of the world has a hot climate, which is good for growing maize. Beans also grow well here.

Maize plant and cob.

Rice plant and grain

Rice field (paddy)

▲ (Picture 2) People who live in southeast Asia might eat this meal. In the warm, wet climate the crop that grows best is rice. Next to the rice are pieces of fish and slices of green peppers. The fish are often kept in the flooded fields and canals where the rice grows. Ducks, for meat, can also be reared in the same place.

▼ (Picture 3) These are steamed bananas wrapped up in a banana leaf. This is a meal that is prepared by some people who live in central Africa. In this part of the world, many people rely on the enormous variety of natural fruits that grow throughout the year. To go with this they may have a porridge made from maize.

Banana plant in tropical rainforest

Summary

- There are many healthy ways to eat.
- Traditional meals are based on food that is grown or reared locally.

Weblink: www.CurriculumVisions.com

Flavoursome food at home

We also have traditional foods which have tasty flavours and keep us healthy.

Just like other parts of the world, we have a range of traditional foods. These are based on the kinds of crops we can grow and the animals we can rear (Pictures 1 and 2). We are also surrounded by the sea, so we can include a wide variety of seafood too.

▼ (Picture 1) This meal might be eaten by people who live in Europe, Australasia or North America. This meal contains a slice of fried lamb, slices of fried potato and peas. It contains things we can grow in our soil and rear on our fields.

Peas in pod

Potato tubers

(Picture 2) All the ingredients of this hamburger are traditional, but they used to be put on a plate. Now they are put together to make a hamburger. This hamburger, for example, contains a bun, which is a CEREAL (just like bread), meat, slices of cucumber, tomatoes and leaves of lettuce (which are fruits and vegetables).

Bitter

Sour

Salty

Sweet

(Picture 3) We taste food through special places on our tongues. Here you can see which parts of the tongue taste which type of flavour. Taste is one of our senses.

Why we like food

The foods we enjoy most are those that have lots of different **FLAVOURS**. On your tongue are special places that are sensitive to sweet things, sour things, bitter things and salty things (Picture 3). We enjoy a meal best if it has some of these flavours.

Making meals tasty

We need food to live, and we get most of our needs from foods that are bulky, like potatoes or bread. But many of the main foods we need are quite dull to eat on their own. Dry bread, for example, is very boring to eat. But if you add jam, it becomes much more attractive. Jam contains lots of sugar, so it tastes sweet.

Crisps on their own are also quite boring, but they taste better when they have salt or vinegar on them, or when other flavours are added.

The sauces we put on our food – such as tomato ketchup – are also designed to make food tasty. Many of the sauces we use contain salt (salty), sugar (sweet) and vinegar (sour) in them. Pickles are another way to give foods more flavour.

Summary
- We eat food because it tastes nice.
- Our mouths contain taste buds that make us want to eat food.
- Adding flavours makes food more attractive to eat.

Weblink: www.CurriculumVisions.com

Foods that do the same job

There are many different kinds of foods, but they can all be placed into just five easy-to-remember groups.

When you looked at the meals on the previous pages, you probably looked at them and thought, "Rice is a **CEREAL**, peas are a **VEGETABLE**", and so on.

What you have done is to put foods into common groups, the same sort of groups you find set out in a supermarket.

This tells us that although many foods and meals look different, they are basically made up of the same kinds of food.

Food groups

All foods can be put into just five food groups: vegetables, **FRUIT**, cereals, meat (including fish) and eggs, and **DAIRY PRODUCTS** (food made with milk).

You can see them arranged on these pages.

Making meals from food groups

We make all of our meals from these food groups. But why can't we just eat one kind of food throughout our lives? Why do we need to eat food from each of the groups? To find that out, we need to know what our bodies get from each kind of food, and that is what we will learn on the following pages.

Group 1: Vegetables

Roots, stems and leaves of plants are called vegetables. Most of these parts of a plant are hard and need to be cooked before eating.

Carrots

Greens

Group 2: Fruit

A fruit is usually soft and juicy and has pips (seeds). Many fruits can be eaten without cooking.

Banana

Apple

Weblink: www.CurriculumVisions.com

Group 3: Cereals

Cereals have seeds, which we call GRAINS. They are small and hard. The main cereals are wheat, oats, maize and rice. Wheat, maize, barley and oats are usually ground up before they are cooked.

Bread

White and brown rice

Group 4: Meat and eggs

Beneath an animal's skin is muscle (often called flesh) and bone. The food we call meat is the muscle.

People all over the world eat meat from fish, sheep and chickens. In some parts of the world other animals (such as pigs and cattle) are used for meat as well. Eggs and shellfish – such as prawns and crabs – also fit into this group.

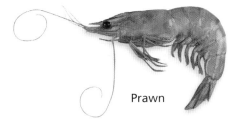
Lamb chop

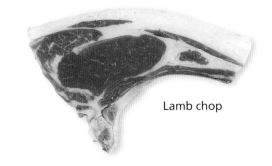
Prawn

Group 5: Dairy products

Dairy products are foods made with milk. They include cream and yoghurt (which are runny), butter (which is soft and easy to spread) and cheese (which is either hard or soft).

Many butter-like spreads, such as margarine, are a mixture of oil and milk, although some contain no milk at all.

Cheese

Milk

Sardine

Eggs

Summary

- Our bodies need a variety of foods to stay healthy.
- The food we eat can be put into five groups: vegetables, fruit, cereals, meat and dairy products.

9

Balancing our food

To get all the nourishment and ENERGY we need, we have to eat a variety of foods. This is called our DIET.

We cannot live without food because food contains all the things we need:

▶ to give us energy

▶ to grow

▶ to repair damaged parts of our bodies.

So although we eat food because we enjoy eating it, we also need to eat food because it is good for us.

Working out the variety we need

The food we normally eat and drink is called our diet (Picture 1). Our diet is usually very varied, as you saw on the last page. It includes meat, vegetables, fruit, cereals and dairy products like milk, as well as water, tea, soft drinks and so on.

Our bodies are very good at sorting out the useful parts of the food we eat from the parts that are not useful. So, if we eat a range of different kinds of food as part of our diet, our bodies will sort out what they want to keep and we will stay healthy.

Cereal and milk

Orange juice

Sandwich with cheese, lettuce and tomato filling

Fruit

Milk

▲▶ (Picture 1) Have you noticed that we normally eat different things at different times of the day? We might have cereal at breakfast, sandwiches at lunch and a bigger meal in the evening. This matches the amount of energy we have used up.

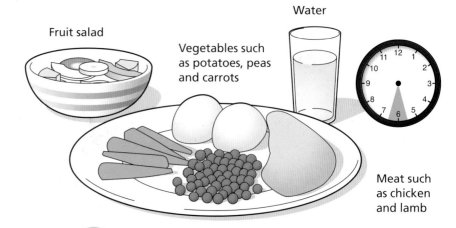

Fruit salad

Vegetables such as potatoes, peas and carrots

Water

Meat such as chicken and lamb

Weblink: www.CurriculumVisions.com

People who are well fed on balanced, nourishing food live longer, can do more work and are stronger than those who do not eat a plentiful, balanced diet.

What people have found from experience is that to get a balanced, nourishing diet we need to eat more of some food groups than others. Picture 2 shows this balance. We need to eat more of the foods from the bottom layers of this diagram, called a food pyramid, and less of the foods from the top.

Drink is a food, too

Our bodies lose water all of the time and this has to be replaced. Some of the water we need comes from our food, but we need to drink liquids as well. Many of these liquids (including water) contain **MINERALS**. Soft drinks contain sugar, and milk contains **VITAMINS** and **FAT**.

Summary
- Our bodies need a variety of foods to stay healthy.
- A diet is the normal foods you eat.
- Drink is a very important part of our diet.

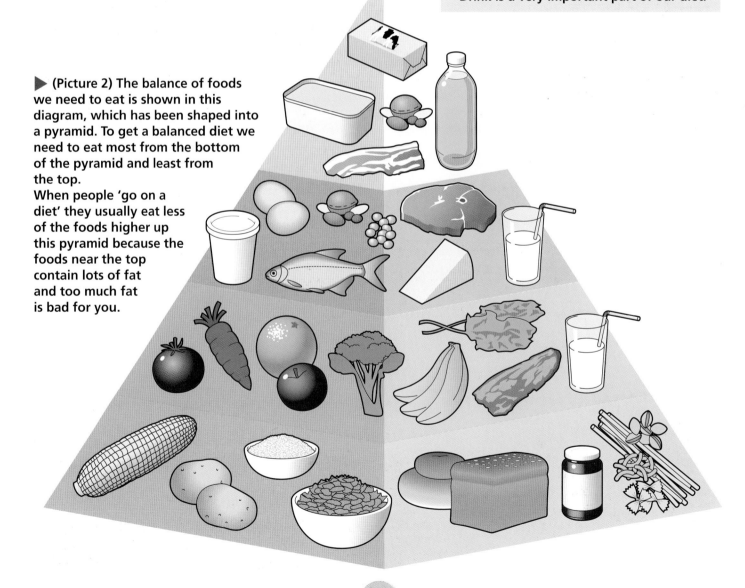

▶ (Picture 2) The balance of foods we need to eat is shown in this diagram, which has been shaped into a pyramid. To get a balanced diet we need to eat most from the bottom of the pyramid and least from the top.
When people 'go on a diet' they usually eat less of the foods higher up this pyramid because the foods near the top contain lots of fat and too much fat is bad for you.

Weblink: www.CurriculumVisions.com

Energy foods

We need three different types of food to give us energy.

We need energy to keep us alive, just as a radio needs batteries to keep it working. We need three kinds of energy: immediate energy, energy to keep us going through the day, and a store of energy just in case we have to go without eating for a long while.

▼ (Picture 1) Fudge is a source of sweet sugar. Sugar provides instant energy and gives a sweet taste.

Sugar

The body uses a special kind of sugar as its source of energy. You might think that we could get all the energy we wanted just by eating spoonfuls of sugar (Picture 1). However, lots of this kind of sugar can be bad for us.

We get most of the sugar we need from a substance called **STARCH**, which is a common part of cereals like rice and wheat and of vegetables like potatoes (Pictures 2 and 3). That is why we should make these kinds of food an important part of our diet.

▼ (Picture 2) These potato 'ghosts' show you two kinds of high energy foods. The potato 'bodies' are packed with starch, and the raisin 'eyes' are really dried grapes that are packed with sugar.

Boiled rice

▶ (Picture 3) A simple test for starch in a food is to boil the food, then pass it through a sieve and collect the liquid. If there is white colouring in the water, starch is present.

Fat

Fat is so packed with energy that we don't need to store much of it. In fact, just a kilogram of fat, spread thinly around our body, can keep us alive without eating for several weeks. Fat comes from the oils in some plants, but especially from meat and dairy products (Picture 4).

You should not eat too much fat. At the same time, most people do not want to stop eating meat. However, lean meat has much less extra fat, and this is the kind most people prefer nowadays.

Many foods give out fat during cooking (Picture 5), so if this is poured away before eating the food (and not mixed with gravy or sauces), you can easily lower the amount of fat you eat.

About four per cent of whole milk is fat, but semi-skimmed milk is only two per cent fat. So, just by changing to semi-skimmed milk, you can eat less fat.

Summary
- We take in energy from food as sugar, as starch and as fat.
- Sugary foods can give a rapid burst of energy.
- Fat is used as a long-term reserve of energy.
- Starch is our main supply of energy.

▶ (Picture 4) Cream contains lots of fat.

▶ (Picture 5) The juices from cooked meat are high in fat.

Weblink: www.CurriculumVisions.com

Body-building foods

The body needs certain materials to make its various parts. These materials can be supplied by both animals and plants.

You need energy to keep going through the day, but you also need materials to build your body, to help you to grow and to replace any parts that get damaged or worn out.

The main substance you need for body-building is called **PROTEIN** (Picture 1).

▶ **(Picture 1)** You don't need to do weight training to build a normal, healthy body – it happens naturally when you eat foods with proteins in them.

Body-building with meat

Meat is packed with proteins. This is why you do not need to eat large amounts of meat to get the materials your body needs (Picture 2). The problem can be that, along with body-building protein, meat also contains too much energy-giving fat.

Body-building with vegetables

You may think that your body needs the flesh of animals to give it enough building materials. But this is not so. In fact, your body breaks down all the food it gets – meat or plant – into tiny 'building blocks' and rearranges them to build parts for your body. That is why you can get all the materials you need from plants. People who only eat plants and no meat are called **VEGETARIANS**.

Many plant seeds, such as beans and peas, contain the same proteins and body-building materials as meat (Picture 3). However, some varieties of plants, such as lentils, peanuts and soy beans, are particularly rich in body-building materials (Picture 4).

So you really do have a choice: meat or plants or both.

▶ **(Picture 2)** You only need to eat a small amount of meat to get all the body-building materials that you need for a day.

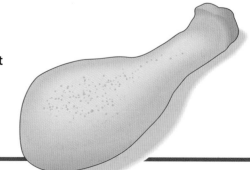

▶ (Picture 3)
This is a vegetarian
meal from south Asia.
Although the meal contains
only vegetables and starch
(rice), it provides plenty of proteins.

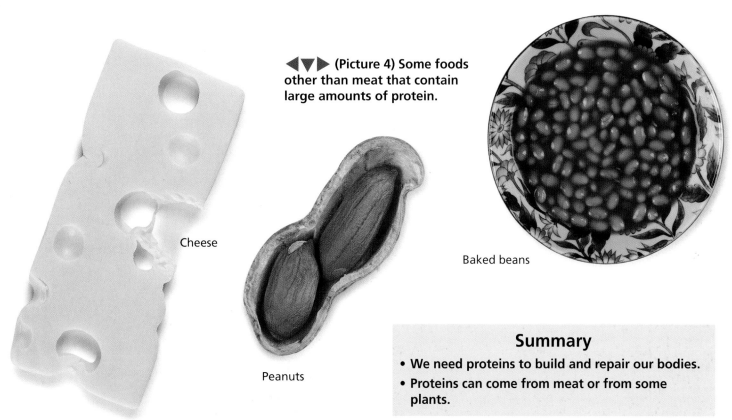

◀▼▶ (Picture 4) Some foods
other than meat that contain
large amounts of protein.

Cheese

Peanuts

Baked beans

Summary
- We need proteins to build and repair our bodies.
- Proteins can come from meat or from some plants.

Teeth

TEETH are vital for breaking up food into the small pieces that the body can use. Each kind of tooth has a special place, and a special shape for the job it has to do.

A tooth is like a peg sticking out of your jaw (Picture 1). You have two sets of teeth. You start to grow the first set – called **MILK TEETH** – when you are about six months old, and start to get the second, and final, set when you are about six years old.

What the teeth do

The teeth break large pieces of food into small pieces so that they can be swallowed easily. To do their job of breaking down food, they have to be hard, specially shaped, and they must not break easily.

There are three different kinds of teeth in your mouth. This is what they do.

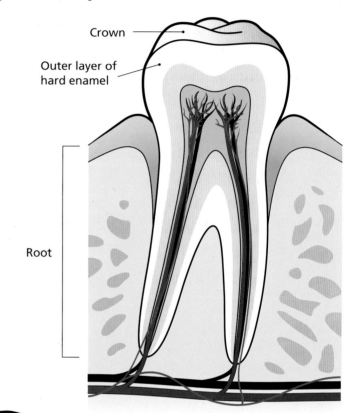

Crown

Outer layer of hard enamel

Root

▲ (Picture 1) A tooth is a living part of the body. If the hard cover, called enamel, rots, the tender inside becomes exposed.

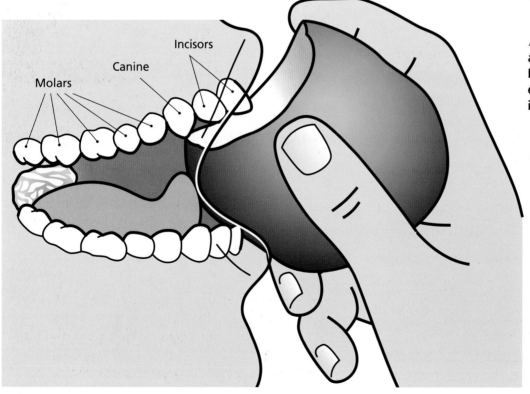

Incisors

Canine

Molars

◄ (Picture 2) The types of teeth in our mouths.

Cutting teeth

The front teeth in your mouth are designed for cutting. They are chisel shaped (Picture 2). This kind of tooth is called an incisor. There are four incisors in the top and bottom set of teeth. They are shaped to cut into food as you bite.

Tearing teeth

Behind the front teeth are teeth with pointed tops. These are called canine teeth. The points are used to tear food into smaller pieces so other teeth can then crush the food.

Grinding teeth

At the back of the mouth there are broad, flattish teeth for crushing and grinding food. They are called molars. These teeth get larger towards the back.

Caring for teeth

Teeth are usually covered in a natural, sticky coating called **PLAQUE**. Sugary foods stick to the plaque, and the plaque changes the sugar into acid. The acids then begin to rot the **ENAMEL** (Picture 3).

The best way to prevent this problem is to eat foods that scrape the plaque off your teeth. Apples and other hard fruit and vegetables will do this, but cleaning your teeth regularly is the most effective thing you can do because the toothpaste also contains a substance that balances out the acid (Picture 4).

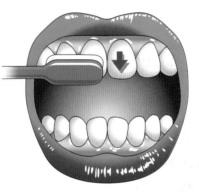
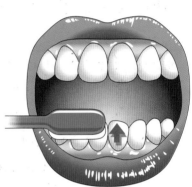

◀ (Picture 3) Tooth decay causes holes to develop in the enamel.

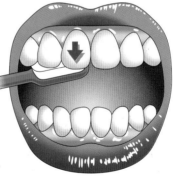
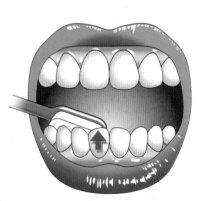

▲ (Picture 4) How to brush your teeth to remove as much plaque as possible.

Summary
- Your teeth are designed to help you break up and crush your food.
- Teeth can become damaged if they are covered in plaque.
- Cleaning your teeth protects them from decay.

Weblink: www.CurriculumVisions.com

What do wild animals eat?

All animals have their own form of balanced diet. Some eat meat, plants or a mixture of the two. Few can eat the same food as we do.

Wild animals are very sensible about what they eat. Just like us, they sense that some foods are good for them. They know that their bodies can only digest certain foods. This is why animals search for the foods that suit them best. If it cannot find suitable food, an animal will starve, even if there are other types of food around.

Plant eaters

Many animals can only get their proper diet by eating plants (Picture 1). Some of the world's largest animals, such as the elephant and the giraffe, are plant eaters.

There are large numbers of plant eaters in every part of the world. These may be insects such as grasshoppers, seed-eating birds such as finches, or small animals such as squirrels and beavers (Picture 2) which eat fruits, nuts and the bark from trees.

Meat eaters

Some animals can only get their proper food by eating other animals (Picture 3).

We tend to think of meat eaters as large animals such as lions and tigers. But smaller animals, such as frogs and hawks, are meat eaters, too. Such animals cannot use plants for food because they cannot digest plants.

Meat and plant eaters

Only a few animals can get nourishment from both plants and other animals. The bear and the wild boar are two animals that eat both meat and plants.

▼ **(Picture 1) This is the skull of a deer. Deer feed entirely on plants and need to be able to cut and grind the tough fibres in their food.**

The incisors and canines are only present in the lower jaw. The upper jaw has a tough pad. The teeth and the pad act like a knife and chopping board when the animal bites grass. The back teeth have many ridges which grind up the food as the jaw moves from side to side.

Molars

Incisors and canines

Weblink: www.CurriculumVisions.com

The beaver is capable of cutting down trees just by eating through them, as this picture shows.

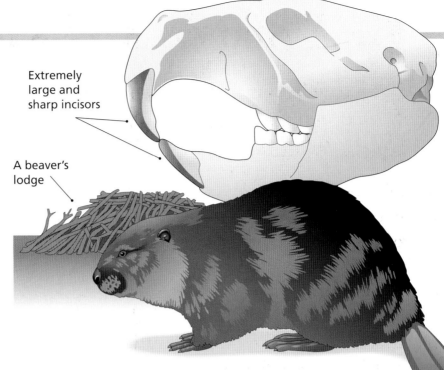

Extremely large and sharp incisors

A beaver's lodge

▲ (Picture 2) The beaver is a type of animal called a rodent. Other rodents include rats, hamsters and guinea pigs.

The front teeth of rodents are self-sharpening. The front of their incisors have a hard enamel layer that wears down more slowly than the rest of the tooth leaving a sharp, cutting edge. These teeth grow continuously to keep pace with the wear and tear they get from tough food.

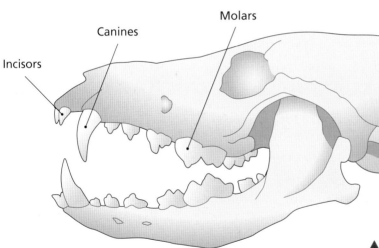

Molars

Canines

Incisors

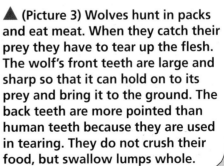

▲ (Picture 3) Wolves hunt in packs and eat meat. When they catch their prey they have to tear up the flesh. The wolf's front teeth are large and sharp so that it can hold on to its prey and bring it to the ground. The back teeth are more pointed than human teeth because they are used in tearing. They do not crush their food, but swallow lumps whole.

Summary

• Plant-eating animals have teeth designed for crushing and grinding.

• Meat-eating animals have teeth designed for holding and tearing.

• Some animals can eat both plants and other animals.

Weblink: www.CurriculumVisions.com

What should pets eat?

Pets should eat similar foods to their wild relatives if they are to stay healthy.

A pet such as a cat or a dog is a tame animal. But thousands of years ago their ancestors were not tame. They were wild animals. People tamed them and made them into pets because they were useful. Dogs were good protection and cats hunted rats and other animals that carry disease.

Pets are not humans. Their insides are different and they need a different range of food from humans.

A dog's diet

Although dogs will eat scraps from the table, this is not their proper food. Some human foods can actually harm pets.

Some dogs, for example, can be made very ill if given chocolate.

The wild relatives of the dog were probably wolves. Wolves are meat eaters, so pet dogs should be given at least some meat to eat (Picture 1). They can also be given special biscuits for added nourishment.

Cat food

Cats are meat eaters. They cannot get any nourishment from plants and so they must be given meat (Picture 2).

Because it senses that it needs meat, your cat may still hunt birds and mice even though you may give it all the food it needs.

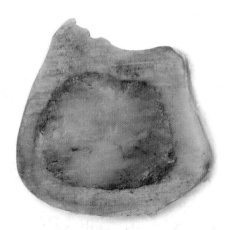

(Picture 1) Bones are a source of food for dogs. When a dog has finished ripping the meat from a bone, it will crack the bone open. Inside the bone is soft marrow which is rich in nourishment.

ink: www.CurriculumVisions.com

Rabbits, hamsters and the like

Rabbits, guinea pigs and hamsters (Picture 3) can be fed on vegetables, such as carrots and cauliflower, but they still need grass every day, even if it is in the form of dried grass called hay. The hay contains fibre which helps them digest their food. They will also eat a mixture of cereals.

Remember the water

All pets need water as well as food for their diet, and, if you keep a pet, you should make sure that it is able to take a drink at any time.

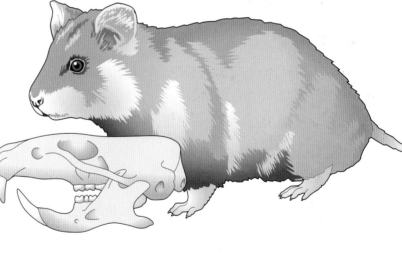

▼ (Picture 2) Cats have large canine teeth for tearing into flesh. The sharp incisors cut flesh from bone. The back teeth have pointed ends for holding flesh as the incisors cut it. Cats do not have flat crushing teeth.

▲ (Picture 3) Hamsters and rabbits have continuously growing teeth to cope with the tough plant food they have to eat. That is why, if you do not give them naturally tough food to eat, you need to provide them with wooden twigs or something similar to help them file down their teeth.

Summary
- Pets are descended from wild animals.
- Pets need to be given the same sort of food as their wild relatives.
- Pets can be harmed by eating human food.

Weblink: www.CurriculumVisions.com

Index

Science@School

Teacher's Guide

There is a Teacher's Guide to accompany this book, available only from the publisher.

There's much more on-line including videos

You will find multimedia resources covering this and ALL 37 QCA Key Stage 1 and 2 science units as well as history, geography, religion and spelling subjects in the Professional Zone at:

www.CurriculumVisions.com

A CVP Book
Copyright © 2002–8 Earthscape

First reprint 2003. Second reprint 2005. Third reprint 2008.

The right of Brian Knapp to be identified as the author of this work has been asserted by him in accordance with the Copyright, Designs and Patents Act 1988.

All rights reserved. No part of this publication may be reproduced, stored in a retrieval system, or transmitted in any form or by any means, electronic, mechanical, photocopying, recording or otherwise, without prior permission of the copyright holder.

Author
Brian Knapp, BSc, PhD

Educational Consultant
Peter Riley, BSc, C Biol, MI Biol, PGCE

Art Director
Duncan McCrae, BSc

Senior Designer
Adele Humphries, BA, PGCE

Editor
Lisa Magloff, MA

Illustrations
David Woodroffe

Designed and produced by
EARTHSCAPE

Printed in China by
WKT Co., Ltd

Volume 3A *Food, teeth and eating*
– Curriculum Visions Science@School
A CIP record for this book is available from the British Library.

Paperback ISBN 978 1 86214 100 1

Picture credits
All photographs are from the Earthscape Picture Library.

This product is manufactured from sustainable managed forests. For every tree cut down at least one more is planted.